A CORPSE IS ALSO A GARDEN

a corpse is also a garden

PIETER MADIBUSENG ODENDAAL

poems translated from the Afrikaans by the poet

uhlanga

2025

a corpse is also a garden
© Pieter Madibuseng Odendaal, 2025, all rights reserved

First published in Durban, South Africa by uHlanga in 2025
UHLANGAPRESS.CO.ZA

Distributed outside South Africa by the African Books Collective
AFRICANBOOKSCOLLECTIVE.COM

ISBN: 978-1-0370-5173-9

Edited by Marike Beyers and Nick Mulgrew

Cover design by Jennifer Jacobs
Cover image: "Hazelnut (male flower), overlay of 7 channel autofluorescence microscopy", by ZEISS Microscopy, September 20, 2016; used under a Creative Commons licence, CC-BY 2.0

Typesetting by Nick Mulgrew
Proofread by Karina Szczurek

The body text of this book is set in Garamond Premier Pro

ACKNOWLEDGEMENTS

Thank you to Marike Beyers who edited the English translations, and to Jorge Alejandro Ccoyllurpuma for being my first and most avid reader.

The poems in this collection had their first lives in the Afrikaans collections *asof geen berge ooit hier gewoon het nie* (2018) and *Ontaard* (2023), both published by Tafelberg Uitgewers.

"On the crowded hills of Makhanda" first appeared on natureislouder.com.

"the night the sea sang" is based on a translation by Annel Pieterse, from *ConVerse: Contemporary South African Poets in Translation* (2018), published by InZync Poetry and Woordfees.

CONTENTS

river mouth   *12*
the night the sea sang   *14*
so they who are no longer them   *16*
twin   *17*
everything happens all at once   *18*
scenes from a gay childhood   *21*
bath   *tsunami*   *24*
initiation   *26*
north namibia   *27*
pa is sleeping   *29*
the first stone   *30*
against pieter odendaal   *33*

🕪

for mzansi   *35*
elm tree   *39*
when the world nears its end   *41*
in praise of protest   *43*
cape prayer   *44*
eerste rivier   *46*

🕪

late-night stranger   *50*
suddenly spotlights   *52*
we who remain   *54*
PS (where you return to comfort me)   *57*
turning tails   *58*
now that my days   *59*
escape, ethekwini   *61*

shirtless elder   *63*
turn into sea   *64*

◉

the first half of the year is gone   *66*
stream   *67*
when you swim backwards   *68*
physiology lab   *69*
the student returns to his desk   *70*
freelance muse   *71*
if all my lovers   *72*
the world is wide and full of longing   *73*
day of goodwill   *74*
honeymoon   *75*

◉

cleansing   *78*
The greatest hunt in history   *80*
on the crowded hills of Makhanda   *82*
stoke   *87*
flakes   *89*
the most carefree dream about my dad in years   *90*
to my parents   *91*
disappear   *92*
mountain indaba   *93*
ode to air   *95*
if I wake before I die   *96*
a corpse is also a garden   *97*

dedicated to the memory of my uncle, Thomie Holtzhausen

*The land does not belong to us, we belong to the land.
That is the real homesickness,
and that is the proprietorship of the dead.*

– Anne Michaels, *The Winter Vault*

*"What were you before you met me?"
"I think I was drowning."
"And what are you now?"
"Water."*

– Ocean Vuong, *On Earth We're Briefly Gorgeous*

river mouth
milnerton beach

I am a gathering of waters
a meeting of salt and fresh
where oystercatchers gulls & humans
stream through the tides
where rivers seek the ocean
and waves need land
always unfinished   tempestuous mouth

table bay lies between the mountain and me
the detached city blooms buildings
built to bury the water
but the sea remembers
the ships full of slaves and masters
who came here to quench their thirst
after months of salt and sweat
who came to wash and forget

I see two ships
en route to the cape
the one from the north
an odendaal on deck
VOC soldier willem adriaan
mutating in my cells

the second from madagascar
diana trapped in the bow
bound along with other unblessed ones
for bowing and yes-mams
she bears her baas' child: susanna
thrives despite the blood
marries willem adriaan
ma diana disappears
odendaals flood the land

I am a gathering of waters
a meeting of salt and fresh
where oystercatchers gulls & humans
stream through the tide
where rivers seek the ocean
and waves need land
always unfinished   tempestuous mouth

the night the sea sang

> *and the water, restless, wishes it could spew*
> *all the slaves and ships onto shore*
>
> – Koleka Putuma, "Water"

I lie half-awake half-drunk
against a dune on bloubergstrand
the city floats
        phosphor on the sea
the mountain lacerates the night

a crowd rises from the sea
between me and robben island
the aquatic choir comes up for air
their heads buoyed by the waves
senzeni na! they gurgle from their throats

the halfmoon is a white judge
like the truth about this world:
we conquer each other like giant ants
we seethe across the land
the earth oozes violence

silenced generations trail
across the broken shells
way back to autshumao
in the night that knows no colour

their skins are peeled peaches
hair strung from seaweed and sand
cheeks and guts hollowed into grottos
for furious crabs and anemones to hide

brine streams from their lips
inscribing their stories on the water
the sea shudders with meaning

so they who are no longer them
for grandpa piet

my ancestors surround me
in each breath I take
in the wild grass   the summers
and the aurora lights
in the heavens of my brain

they return to the atmosphere
when their carbon chains
decouple and disperse
like water evaporating
from the sea

they weave themselves
back into the world
they diffuse into the day
and I see through them
I carry my ancestors on my face

a collage of my origins
the same ones that surround me
so they who are no longer them
can meet themselves through my eyes
in the wind

twin

it's three in the morning   you're my prehistory
we return to the mother
head-against-toe in her dark water:
three hearts beating in an ocean of flesh

your mouth lies in me   I drank all of you
our DNA and all your breaths
in those ten weeks
mom insists her womb
was too small for two

you'll show me death's way   I know
you're the elsewhere keeping me awake
to write these words   perhaps
you'd hate the world anyway

or did I outmanoeuvre you?   you're my remorse
for now I rest in the shade of eucalyptus
and my man's soiled hands   we grow
mealies and potatoes   lack nothing

all the clouds and holy rocks know about you
and your mom and brother who grew old without you
I carry you   I salve you   we sleep in the ravines
at sunrise the river floats you home

everything happens all at once

it's winter or summer
everything happens all at once
and never ends

we live on a plot
with rabbits and hadedas
tomatoes, strawberries, onions

*

our maths teacher drops us off
at the skew gate
after parents' night
and pa's too many drinks
boetie grinds his teeth
like the wheels on the gravel driveway

dankie meneer, I mumble
rush to open the door
we carry pa together
away from the brights
and into the yard

*

pa sleeps weeks away in bed
the sun drags through the sky
shadows drag across the land
that he knows he is losing
he wanted to give us the veld of his childhood

mom leaves their door ajar
he wilts in quiet shafts of light

*

he parties in welkom
clings to the wheel
and the white line of night
his car somersaults into a mealie field
everything shatters except him

next morning bible study in bed
mom dredges up the wreck
I pray and thank jesus
that the earth didn't crush pa
like it did the bakkie

and can someone help me
pick the rotting strawberries
please   amen

*

pa's glasses lie in his lap
he picks the shards from his eyes
quiet as a bomb

it's winter or summer
everything happens all at once
and never ends

scenes from a gay childhood
or, how I learnt to swear

we change into red speedos
before PE next to the pool
the boys cluck around the slit
between us and the girls' change rooms
        I'm quite happy with my surrounds

        *

somewhere in pre-primary
almost drowned out
but his name started with an m or n

we show our planets to each other
in the last toilet stall
the most natural thing on earth

        *

I saunter past the boys in the sun after break
shiny ties short grey shorts someone shouts   *pieter, guys!*
    asses against the wall!
        the line bursts into laughter
their mouths shatter everywhere

        *

our hands feed the current around our bodies
in his parents' pink bath
his gums the colour of dusk when he laughs

I hide somewhere behind his eyes   until the cold
crumples our toes and fingers into maps

*

we roll tea leaves in toilet paper   proudly light them in the toaster
our lungs regret it instantly   my ex is your girlfriend
we lie next to each other   and far away from ourselves
hold each other's curled pinkies   in the longest greenest shadow
on the dirt-green lawn   in the backyard of my youth

*

I sprint home
bag slicing through my collarbones
someone shouted *faggot* in class
I ask jesus to forgive me I shout
fuck fucking mother
mother fucking mother fucker!
for the first time in my life

the wind hurls my screams
and the boys' frozen hearts
down the avenue of leafless trees
where you don't come to find me

*

I tighten the tie striped around my neck
        tears of laughter
for the freedom in my mouth

bath

the water is a monk
raking the sand of my skin
I'm his meditation garden

his consistent grooves peacefully
line my feet and fingers

I kiss him with an open mouth
my breath liquifies

tsunami

he explodes in blue
against the sweating day
his bald head a furious moon
his white cloth wipes out suburbs

he yanks buildings out like weeds
roads curl and whip
cars forget the weight of steel

waves crash through our cursed bodies
  in their wake
    exhausted mouths
    erring hands
    the false steps of our feet

pa shakes me back from the pit
he scares away the flood

I cough up salt from my lungs
the world keeps on breaking

initiation

we drive through the heart
of the kalahari on the back of a 4x4
the wind curls through our hair
grass billows like a warning

a herd of springbuck huddle up ahead
I press the butt against my shoulder
pa's advice in my ear
we stop
        the grass sings
                      I take aim
the shot slices through the morning

I hit his back leg
he limps away from death

we drive to the brink of my manhood
flickering in the sun
writing his bloody poem in the sand

come on, son
        you must slit his throat
                otherwise he'll suffer

I dip my fingers in the ink
take his head in my hands
avoid everything in his eyes

north namibia

> *agter ons lê brand en verwoesting*
> *lê blinde vrouens en verbete kinders*
> *lê ons skadu en almal weet dis ons*
> *ons drink droë water en ons lag*
>
> – Wopko Jensma, "Ons wreek ons"

thousands of stones scattered around us
like curious eyes   *k▆▆brak*
pa mumbles through his beard
when we pass a road stall

the ribbed canine chews a dry lizard
wide-eyed ovambos stare at our bakkie
an eager son runs closer to invite us
pa stares down the road

    pa, I ask
        yes

the stall disappears in the rear-view mirror
stones pack the sky
one day everything will be desert
we, the ovambos, the bakkie, the mongrel and the lizard
will lie windswept beneath the sand

pa
on the border
did you ever
you know

        no

his fingers clasp the steering wheel
our bakkie sandpapers the landscape to dust

pa is sleeping

pa is sleeping next to me on the couch
the last two cream shirt buttons undone

his stomach protrudes like a struggle song
against the darkness ahead

he sings as he snores
rubs his feet together exactly like me

his glasses cling to his ears
his breath clings to his lips

the first stone
for adam small

I wish I lived a stone's throw
from you, mister small
from the benches the doors
the trains the schools the beaches
the riots the casting of stones

but I tread on the other side of the storm
where we project rainbows onto
the gray screens of our days

you can't build a life
on rocks made of air

I don't know how
to write to you from here
where blind youngsters dance
with iPods in their ears
dollars in their eyes

you can't build a life
on rocks made of air

I wish I was born earlier
that I could walk the day Hector fell
perhaps I could have carried him
perhaps I would also have played
cowboys and crooks

but my hands have always been
too small to throw stones
despite oupa's senate speeches
and dad's dark blood
oupa died the year when
dad went to the border

my dad is a good man, mister small
even though his eyes are always sheltering from war
even with his brandy breath
he's a good man, mister small
even though he curses at taxis
and serves a god who condoned it all

he's a good man, mister small
and I hope that one day I will stand
free from shame
when I cry at his grave

against pieter odendaal
for pieter odendaal

i. prologue

I no longer pin my name to my chest
I hide the letters like bones in my pockets
so I can show you exactly
when you ask me where I'm from

(may the poem absolve
the dead from the spectacle)

ii. the charge

in the spring of my eleventh year
pieter odendaal clamps john rampuru's
ankles to the back of his bakkie at midnight
with the wire he strings into fences

odendaal was drunk and medicated
he can't recall the events of that evening
the judge decides in steel-cold afrikaans

the rampurus catch words where they can
in the chicken-wire sieve of their comprehension

police wrap the courthouse in barbed wire
people toyi-toyi down the road
where john's dried blood trailed for days

the back of his head was a pulp
the buttocks had been worn away
by the dragging along the asphalt
the lower legs of his overalls
were the only thing left on his body

pieter paid him R800 a month
    couldn't speak to us like a human being
john's brother remembers
    he always made noise when talking

odendaal got ten years, three suspended,
after hauling john for five kilometers
through the lightless streets of sasolburg
because pieter can't recall, you see
he simply can't recall

in my matric year
john's flesh had long fled his bones
pieter snored, a shotgun next to his bed,
dreaming of all the fences
he'd erect across the land

    odendaal, hear me now
    I'll pass you on the street
    without a flinch
    I write you off
    I cleanse my name
    scour until my back
    blooms pink carnations

for mzansi
a "dialogue" in 180 voices from commentaries on a News24 article

remember
>*i don't think i have to*

you need to get off your high horse
broer
>*sorry baas that i am so ignorant*

no doubt you think a necklace
is simply a fun piece of jewellery
why don't you bring your face closer

i remember
being able to identify
landmines limpet mines makarov pistols
before I was 10
i remember
when our family couldn't enter
shops and restaurants through the same
door
i remember
the day i saw black
people dressed like whites
walking on the beach at scottburgh
i went to public school
just as they did
i held my school shoes together
with elastic bands
>*yes we have a kak past*
>*but we are not a bitter and twisted people*
>*blacks had their homelands whites had theirs*

did van riebeeck come to africa
carrying land in his ships?

i lived here with a heart
people forced me to hide it
i had to leave through a choice of my own
> *i was 7 my brother 4 when we*
> *became a democratic republic*
> *i did not commit atrocities*
> *neither did my brother*
> *all we got was a stab in the back*

> *most white saffers*
> *would be happy to work under a black government*
> *so easy on us whiteys we want the same things*
> *but build a city before you rename our streets*

they built your country
with their sweat and tears
black people were very forgiving
a bit too much perhaps
they will be afraid to walk on the streets
cowards that they are
> *ek's trots om 'n wit suid-afrikaner*
> *te wees*

eish dis langwij of da umlungu
is cunfushesing although
the bit I know helps a lot to hear
when they are talking about me

always remember that when talking behind our backs
> *at least there's dialogue*

talk is different from vomiting
be silent oh ignorant one

no pissies have ever come from south africa
let's look at the facts
st. james' church kenilworth 25 july 1993
they threw grenades and opened fire
on the congregation killing 11 wounding 58
    laundry and ironing done
    meals prepared
    lawns mowed
    my domestic
bless her soul
    was on her way from work
    when she was pulled into a shack
    and raped by 4 men for 3 days
    she died a year ago
8 january 1982 koeberg nuclear power plant
    a child was set on fire whilst alive
mothers killed taking children to school
    some had their fingers cut off
car bomb nedbank square building church street
4.30 pm on a friday
20 ambulances took the dead and wounded to hospital

    no place like home!
an eye for an eye?
    blah blah sob sob
    cry us a river
why don't you
cry the beloved country?

> *why don't you*
> *move to the zimbabwe ruins?*

we will grow old here
> *the old folks*
> *need to let go and get over it*
> *it makes it harder for us*
> *to correct your mistakes*

maybe if your grandparents were almost beaten to death
for a slice of chocolate cake
you would also be angry
regardless of what language their screams were in
you are a beneficiary of apartheid
whether you like it or not
do you?
> *i don't know*

what is wrong with our skin?
> *i don't know*

what colour is our blood?
> *i don't know*

i just hope we don't pass this on
> *to our children*

it'll take a while
> *peace my bra*

it'll take a while
> *nuff said*

elm tree

I estimate your perimeter
break ground where the green begins
your trunk is pulverised around the fissure
– surefire signs of suffering – the previous
owners wanted shade for their 70s children
one evening you tumbled to rest on the patio roof

for days I dig to exhume your heart
with spade and pick and rake and trowel
over under and between your limbs
sunlight and breath knotted into gnarls
I comb lumps of earth from your hair
empty the spaces between your roots
your coral body bakes dry in the sun

I attack you piecemeal with my father's axe
kick you open, yellow sawdust round my ankles,
shoulder and back contracting from the arch

and the pick and the arch and the pick
a fistful of ground shoots through the air
earthworms squirm in the excavated earth

I gleefully break you in two like bread
throw the last of your body over my shoulders
at night I scrub the soil from my nails
earth water whirlpools down the drain, I go to bed

my hands still clinging to the tools in the moonlight,
cold and innocent, encircling the hole

it would fit me
perfectly

when the world nears its end

and winter rain occupies bloemfontein
I listen while the muted day
replays against my eyelids
to the waves of raindrops on zinc
chanting protests

how many litres has the sky
poured out onto this land?
why is the soil still so red?

weak acid patters away cars and cables
the clouds strike thunderbolt retributions
drops of rain salve my neighbour's bare feet on his stoep
showing him what forgiveness feels like

how many litres has the sky
poured out onto this land?
why is the soil still so red?

I hear the water's breath
sifting through the photons of streetlights
the tired dance on middle-class roofs
the trickling and trampling in gutters
the whirlpools down drains
swallowing all sound

how many litres has the sky
poured out onto the land?
why is the soil still so red?

elsewhere
beyond the rain
another me stands
      cupped ears under quiet stars
waiting with the land
for the wind to turn

in praise of protest
utopia burns badly baby

if the heat scorches us
we'll all be the same shade
– seared mountain face –
fynbos blooms best after the flame

cape prayer

bless the fat-ass kings
who dance on the heads of workers
buried waist-deep in the ground
trowels in hand to patch up
the rotting partitions

bless the tightly strung wires
keeping export grapes from ailing hands
and the land we still don't own
where our grandparents decompose

bless the tiktok videos
on police violence and infant rape
the shosholozas
the waka-waka ey-eys
the de-la-rey de-la-reys
in the stadiums of catharsis
where we rejoice in brain-damaged men
in pt shorts who fuck each other up
like it's the good old days

bless the searing histories
encircling us like bushfires
the lack of running water
we can't use to douse the flames
and the few who own the forest

for our children who lose their heads
young as the morning
for our elders who dream
of a time when hearts were holy
and the tightening of aortas
around necks like rope
for our dead who toyi-toyi
through the streets of our sleep

bless those who still scrub their innocent hands
and the controlling cronies who cordon off valleys
and spit-roast our fat-fed dreams
over the flaming hearts of fallen heroes

in the name of our futile forefathers
amen

eerste rivier
stellenbosch

i.
here where the eerste rivier awakes
at the first waterfall in jonkershoek
the water chants an ode to gravity
wind-swept mist touches my face
algae and grass droop
like paused rain along the cliff

the ecosystem's throat spreads
rumours through the valley
coils through stellenbosch
and empties itself in macassar
into the primordial source

follow me
as I turn my back on the falls
and walk along the stream
it's october, the ericas bloom
compound pink in the sun
a trio of hadedas flies past
can you hear the wind
reaping all stories and sound
weathering them away
in the folds of mountains?

   ii.
we catch up with our palaeolithic ancestors
strolling beside the river: a dead duiker draped
across the hairy man's shoulders
his daughter drags patterns
with a stick in the sand
a duet between her and the soil
we flow past the unmarked khoi graves
their spirits seep into the river
the water remembers everything

simon named you eerste rivier
he obviously saw you first
glib gables bloom white in the morning
a slave is hanged for arson on the square
we flow past

   iii.
once you streamed the town together
churned the mills fed the farms
now they feed you pesticide

river-dwellers call you shelter
exuberant backyards tumble onto you
history reeks of the human shit
left like beacons on your bank
cyclists and joggers speed past

now we are in the town proper
human sounds displace your song
you merge with the plankenburg
beneath the bridge at bosman's crossing
where you can taste the change in colour
kayamandi's dreck darkens the water
even the united waterfall
reflects our abject separation
we flow past

   iv.
I put my ear against your bank in the dusk
where drifters hang their washing on branches
listen how the day's sounds
mowers cars spades trains
all fade into you

hoor die rivier die rivier was eerste hier

she carries the stories of generations
spuming over stones
we are always underway
one day we'll flow back to the sea
to remind the waves that gravity
herds all streams into rivers

hoor die rivier die rivier was eerste hier

late-night stranger
corridor's stoep, stellenbosch
[to be read aloud with jon hopkins's "abandon window" in the background]

kayamandi stretches before us
the shiny innards of a cow
you live on the other side
where houses are made of bricks,
your slurring tongue assures me
your head is freshly shaven
first your mom, then your dad
at least he left some money for vegetables,
you say, *vir my en buti wam*

you're barely sixteen
twintig, you lie
I don't know how to be a father, I reply
our dishonesty ages us

words stumble between languages
like your drunken ideas about privilege
I stutter half sentences
attempt to anchor
this sinking conversation

nee, jy hoef nie Afrikaans
ja, ek is, maar

your face wavers between me and the shacks
you aim the grain of your mouth
I should dodge, but I set like mud

marry me, you say

never have the stars been scattered so sparsely
across the nightshade sky

suddenly spotlights

the night stuck to me like a corduroy skinny
as our shadows rose and fell beneath streetlights
your breath in my neck bravado in my walk
        too many black labels

we scaled the fence at paul roos high
my skinnies caught the wire
massive hedge-tear on my ass
crossed the glittering rugby field
to that unlit stage of chlorine-bright water
        polo goals in the wings

the stars gathered to see us play
we peeled off each other's clothes
our hands sculpting us
into who we wanted to be

        last one in is a loser!

we dove into baptism
multiplying our movements
the rowing oars of your arms
the fishing rod of your arched back
our torsos floating together
        groins raging underwater

suddenly spotlights flooded the pool
a security guard grumbling
>   *you can't do that here!*
we scrambled from our liquid trance
ran from ourselves and the man in the van
back into the darkness
where no one would stop us from fishing

we who remain
for H

I found out the other day
you've been dead for a year

at varsity we were invisible
to each other and ourselves
backpackers on opposite sides of an island
encircled by an unholy ocean of ideas

> *I smell the sunlight in your hair*
> *you hear red helicopters on the roof*
> *your curtains shelter you from the light*
> *I hold your drenched body like a promise*
>
> *your heart flees*
> *a rambling dove*
> *your rocks turn to sand*
> *my ears to question marks*
>
> *the scratches on your arms and neck*
> *the crickets leaping through your skull*
> *the dying leaves on the trees behind res*
> *crumple and crash down*
> *like your mouth*

at the shofar hub on campus
newly-converted first years
laid their dogged hands on you
one queen said you were possessed
you'd tried to get into a stranger's car
when they saved you for the lord
I cursed and took you back to res

> *clouds wring themselves out*
> *lightning cracks across your forehead*
> *you distort, scribble codes in your book*
> *but you can't pin down the night*
> *your shadow flies into the window*

I took you to hospital
your mom's eyes hesitated
I passed you some dunhill blues
we held you up around the steel bed

they sent you home with pills and a request
to visit the clinic next time instead
I cuddled you, tried to translate you

we drove through the night to your parents' house
you took us to a lake
stumbled out to cry among the pine trees on the shore

in kleinmond's main road
you tried to jump out of the car
orange lights barked ballistic

I sang *don't worry about a thing*
we stopped in front of your house
dropped you off forever

PS (where you return to comfort me)

your words forge their own path
among the blue lines of old letters
at the bottom of a drawer

you write about the clairvoyant psychologist
your plans to study theology
include the only copy of a thunda.com photo:

>two twenty-year-old troubadours in a stellenbosch bar
>we laugh like we'll never lose the plot
>like peace is a word
>our skulls will know one day

turning tails
for X

you saw armageddon before the rest of us
and took a shortcut home through the tall quiet grass

now that my days

now that my days come and go
in gradients of grey and the endless rain
turns the sky into a slab of cement
it gets harder to wake up
I don't know what day it is
roll over

bed smells like skin breath armpits and groin
my mattress and I are one
a fever dream shakes me awake
the planet is a giant magnet
I'm a sliver of steel
I roll over

I crawl under the covers into the dark tent cavernous blackness
      ah! to be a blind bat
roll over

contorted intestines
if I sleep I'll forget my stomach
phone dead battery flat no lines binding me
just us: me, the bed and my bladder
(this too will pass)
I roll over

miners marching to or from work
tread past my window

I roll over
miners marching to or from
roll over
miners marching marching marching
roll over
(it's worth getting up for this)
I shut the window
trap a hadeda in the sky
angels aren't free because they have wings
walking and flying are the same thing
I slip back into the incubator
still lukewarm
roll over

to sleep is to become stone
to prepare your house
for the big infestation
to morph into dream
and never wake up
I roll over

escape, ethekwini
for thomie

early morning cig butts lie like
abandoned kisses on the deck
the staff (my uncle and his lover)
snore away after 4am closing
the drizzle still glimmers on the railing's lips
in the morning sun that mostly
doesn't shine for us

how many queers clipped off
their accessories last night
before sneaking home
to count stars against the ceiling until dawn
searching for a liveable planet

later your coarse palms
your unending smile
we heave in the darkroom
reach out for something holy
something that will save us
my warm throbbing hero

tonight we drink body shots
our bloodshot eyes see far
our hips become hurricanes
lips pout like raspberries
for a mouth or cigarette

we plummet through the splintered hands
of strangers who love us as little
as we love ourselves

tomorrow we'll cough awake the day
but our hearts refuse to forget the beat
we strut to sweat our shit away

so stand closer
under the disco ball
soon we'll disappear like water
when the sun swallows us whole
and kneads us into clouds

shirtless elder

I can only see the tightly
knotted muscles of his back
his vertebrae lighter than polystyrene

filling his bottle with pure H20
fresh from the source!
next to a plugged-out pinball machine
in the corner of the shop

he feels me looking, turns around
his face a contour map
sorry, sir, I stammer
he returns to the water

now you're still strong and fresh,
he gurgles over the liquid sound
but old age comes
like a recce in the night

he walks to the counter
the bottle a strange bride in his arms
disappears into the sunlight

(to die is to marry water)

turn into sea
byron bay

a busker sings johnny cash, *sunday morning coming down*
        the ever-fuming sea behind him
his guitar simple like the truth

yesterday an old man
        groped me on the nudist beach
                his fingers aching with lust
or maybe it's the open audience
        but my eyes turn into sea

the drunk ahead flings his backpack across his shoulder
        the dad on the sand throws and catches his toddler
                surfers find the swell like compass needles
the busker brings me back to breath

        my eyes undulate
                like the restless past that never ends
so I pray
        for the drunk and the busker and the old man and the sea

the first half of the year is gone

like a half-loaf of bread after lunch for two
like the stinkwood leaves outside my window
and my dreams for these 183 days

we have aged with such haste
each minute filled with breath and waste
(air water food in   air water food out)

we made promises, jokes and enemies
sent whatsapps and please-call-mes
and remixed our days into dreams

we move like waves through time:
my parents breathe heavier
rufus is losing his hair and bark
and my brother's getting married in december

the moon longs for water
pulls us until we break
onto the beaches of these late days
where we linger for a moment like seafoam
before we become see-through
and seep away

stream

perhaps it was an afternoon like this
after mountain rain had fed the vilkanota
with fantasies of ocean when he bloated
his stomach with water

perhaps the veld sang green in polyphony
while the bulrushes paid quiet witness
when your great-grandpa left
half a glass of rum on the bank
before stumbling across the smooth rocks

perhaps a farmer saw him
and thought he was simply
washing away his sorrow
as he sank fully clothed
into the rejoicing water

perhaps he wanted to cross the river
and greet himself on the other side
perhaps he chose the finest afternoon
to catch the sun in his hands
in the blind stream

when you swim backwards
for a coelacanth

when you swim backwards, do your awkward headstands,
you're a slow-mo acrobat without crowd or lights
the black-blue sea your only audience

kilometres above
ice ages came and went
you saw the rise of reptiles,

birds, fuckers, empires,
and still you'll turn your silent tricks
long after our last syllable

when the rest of us bolted to the surface
gasping for air on land
you lay low and pacified the sea

stay away from here
the light will blind you
to the knowledge of night

teach us to live in darkness
to be done with crowds and lights
and how to unravel the rustle
of our dark electric dreams

physiology lab

the tutor handed us microscopes and a section of cardiac muscle
I switched on the light, brought the image into focus:

cells cuddled like lean lovers, nuclei staring into distant light
their mitochondria wormy drumfires setting everything ablaze

I knew your molecules were still trapped in my plasma
your dissolved breath controlled the acidity in my blood

we made circuits of your thighs in the folds of my brain
your hands were remote controls tapping my neurons for joy

after I drew and labelled the fibers of that beatless heart
I strolled into sunlight under the trees' chloroplast green leaves

and with each step you flaked away in dead cells: the traces
of our chemical rendezvous fell around me like microscopic snow

the student returns to his desk

I would like to use this opportunity
to thank your DNA
for its beautiful self-translations
the cells that gather to build you

for the high concentration of melanin
making pebbles of your eyes
the keratin cultivating hairs here and there
your pores and their intoxicating whispers
their breath like goosebumps

let me also thank
your bones for their support –
without them your muscles wouldn't hang
like grapes in the vineyard of your body
and your tendons, those cables surpassing praise
that make you move so flawlessly

and keep me up at night:
the rhythm of your step
the grammar of your distant hands
and your face turning away from mine
like a poem's last line

freelance muse

I open the app after doomscrolling
new variants and hotspots
profile pic: waves of laurel trees
merging into blue

> *wordsmith wanted*
> *worth his weight in wood*
> *self-aware, flame in the mirror*
> *more tongues more fun*

> *meta4s 4 days*
> *no stanzas attached*
> *pair rhyme, cross rhyme, free verse*
> *into onomatopoeia*

I message a quatrain replete with sounds and visions
green afternoons, sidewalks, dust and sweat
bedroom windows crackling in the wind
bodies between sheets far from the golden sun

I shower and wash away the bleak day
wait for my muse to send his pin

if all my lovers

if all my lovers gathered in the same room
the married and unfaithful
the boys and girls poets and musos
in all their wavering glory

would they see the beauty that threads
their hearts together
would they gang up and fuck me up
or embrace each other as friends

could I look them in the eye
without hesitation
when so much of my body
is strewn between their hips

the world is wide and full of longing
australia, south africa, peru

I sit on the front stoep of a relationship in ruins
on an ex-couple's pig farm in the northern rivers
the valleys of trees are wet to the bone
(the last rains before the flames
came to eat the forest)
two magpies stare each other
down in white and black

the yard dog's ashes
lie on the cushion next to me
       a brown snake bit her last week

last night I dried myself
stood there, naked and still in the bathroom,
because the man in bed wasn't you
and I wasn't his ex

it's the diá de los muertos in peru
you play violin at your grandma's grave
I mourn for the dog in the box on the couch
for the pigs next door who need new dads
for the 39 smuggled bodies found in a british van
for the departed dreams of this house
and for you, chiquito, you who remain precisely
as far away from me
as night from day

day of goodwill

we fold underwear in the laundry
yours mine and our husbands'
  the 16th of january, will you guys come?

the tumble dryer's window draws a halo round your head
your eyes are lightless, cold tiles press against my soles
  we would have loved to, it just feels wrong, you know

unfazed, you pass me the washing
the air between us smells like staysoft and let-downs
  you must follow your heart, sus

I walk away not to cry in front of you
leave you behind in the untainted sunlight

honeymoon

the newlyweds celebrate the submission of their 50-page application
at the visa administration company in gqeberha
they greet the frowning faces behind papers in the queue –
zimbabweans, pakistanis, an italian woman with long, pink nails.

they catch a taxi to sardinia bay. canary yellow, turquoise and white scrunched up
plastic bags cling like oversized lingerie to bushes. uvus'abalele,
the radio replies. are the waking ones angels on judgement day?
the shifting dunes swallow the parking lot's trash bins.

they get out, smell the damp salt of aquatic life,
open their mouths to the wind. beyond
the sand mountain the ocean teases her platinum hair.
they throw coins into the water, thank the ancestors

that their burden now belongs to the wind. they wash away
the anxiety of separation, pray for the others still in the queue.
they nap in the shade of a shiny lifeguard cubicle
on steel stilts. the tippex against the window reckons "fuck you".

a green foam enters. the waves print dark arches,
scary fractals on the sand. a brown spongey blanket
lingers in the bay, swimmers run out. the wind brings bad tidings.
the couple walks back along the sand dunes, suffused with microplastic:

parts of pipes and bottles, shredded ice cream tubs.
the slopes shine like a GIF-rainbow bound to death.
the beach is littered with endocrine disruptors,
stabbing grains of fake sand, needles in the wind.

in the parking lot two dozen workers in orange hazmat suits
form a circle around the boss's orders. they'll clean up the spill
to put bread in plastic on the table. one of them spies
the newlyweds slipping away, before the tide comes in.

cleansing
a diary, in gratitude

I wake up with the stars, phahla, take an uber to kwathema. buy two chickens, brown and white. search in vain for the black one I'm supposed to get. my great-grandma's yellow doek covers my legs, next to gogo now in her mazda. we float through nigel, past mine dumps and bushes woven from plastic. rhodes, milner, kruger, the streets proclaim. we wait where the tar becomes dirt road. gogo prays.

we stop next to a bluegum in the veld. I find a stone, she elects an anthill. we hack the brain open, ants bubble up. gogo slits the brown cock's throat, balances his head on the ruined nest. she carves his body open, adds the gall to the muti. throws the rest on the heap, passes me a red bucket. *drink until you are full.* I swallow, stick my crummy fingers down my throat.

everything black and bitter comes out. I wash out my innards, crouch and groan, find the horizon. I take a seat on the corpse and vomit. *don't touch the ground.* my hands rest on my lap. three incisions on my head – one behind each ear, one between the hairs that cover my red birthmark. she pours the muti over me. I sob, she washes and washes. I dismount the hill, gather my clothes. *today we leave the old things behind.* I walk to the car, gogo and buckets in tow. *don't look back, mkhulu.*

*

we drive to the river. a boy's eyes needle through reeds. *there's someone there*, I say. *he is good, mkhulu.* she throws two R2 coins into the water, greets her people. I imitate her. she slaughters the white cock, throws his gall in the bucket. I get undressed, on my haunches in red briefs in front of her in the water. she baptises me, steps back. *take off your underpants, wrap them around a rock and throw them into the river. you leave this here today.*

I implore all the dead ones I know, toss my briefs into the water. barefoot back to the car. the boy from the reeds chases an iridescent black rooster, catches him for gogo. *a gift from your ancestors,* she says. the trees stare until we disappear behind the dumps.

*

I hold the startled chicken while gogo prepares a futha. I sit down naked, surrounded by a reed screen. she pulls a plastic sail over my head, steaming bucket of herbs between my knees. I sweat zealously. she tells me to negotiate with my people about the leaking anthill in my head. I shout. I see god. I confuse and forgive myself.

cement floor, gogo washes me in a tub between red and white candles. my wet fingers kill them one by one. in gogo's indumba, kaross across her shoulders, she prepares more muti. *you are called, mkhulu,* she says. *you will find your way. camagu gogo. camagu mkhulu.*

I greet gogo and the black cockerel. waft across the footpath to the gate. wet spots mark where she blessed the stones before we left, when we were still on our way to the river, when the chickens still clucked and I was rife with dark matter. I latch the gate behind me, the inscrutable world awaits.

The greatest hunt in history
24 August 1860

Moshoeshoe kisses the prince's feet like dried manure
to save his mountain kingdom while the Barolong herd
the animals into Bainsvlei between skulls and sweet thorns

Prince Alfred, pipsqueak, disaster-in-the-making
crosses the Aliwal Hills with his retinue, his horses,
gunpowder, the Bible. Mqhayi would greet him thus:

Gqithela phambili, Thol' esilo,	*Go away, calf of the Big Cow,*
Nyashaz' ekad' inyashaza!	*Destroyer that keeps on destroying!*
Gqitha, uz' ubuye kakuhle,	*Go away, and return sweetly,*
Ndlalifa yelakowethu.	*Devourer of our land.*

the dung prince's wagons infiltrate dusk, Adam Kok
hugs him in Bloem's red streets, Sir Grey drools about chops
fearful hooves trample through Alfred's dreams

*

sun spills like fool's gold across the plain
they scrum the vlei into dust and adrenaline:
lost bontebokke, vindictive wildebeest,
quaggas and zebras crush their neighbours' breastbones
springbucks shrapnel ostriches mangle the veld

thirty thousand trembling hearts in the morning
the Barolong trap the horde of muscle and breath
the prince shoots a wildebeest, the slaughter begins
herds explode calves vanish a hurricane
of flesh neighs and collisions

they stoke lightning on the hills
cordon off exits, stuff loaded guns
in the teen prince's hands: he shoots
and shoots, shoots and shoots; they devour
the earth, and the market pays 3 shillings per hide

the prince stares across the battlefield
a drop of buck blood kisses his ear
five thousand carcasses, manna for the vultures
their horns gored the heavens today: the evening
is a teeming wound of petrified stars

on the crowded hills of Makhanda

> *You filthy remnant of a world.*
> *You filthy small hours. You filthy hate.*
> *It's you, burden of an insult and a hundred years of*
> *the whip.*
>
> – Aimé Césaire, *Return to My Native Land*

I walk through mist across the hills of Makhanda
       in the wind that knows more sadness than peace
       the town bustles behind us
the burnt stumps of pine and eucalyptus
       crouch over   stand still   turn their backs

humanimals tired to death of searching
they shy away when we get close
shift their weight, avert their eyes

elephant ghosts wait in the kloofs for the afternoon to cool
before scouring the fields for their tusks past yellow
explosions of mimosas   blesbok and springbok
peer over ridges searching for their skins
their muscles gleam like aloe blooms
warriors and rhinos hide in thorny thickets
to storm Makhanda's streets at night

*

study the rings of yellowwood trees
        press your nose against the page
                retrace the bloodspoor across the landscape
                        of unsteady feet fleeing empire

*

Makana, you are a battlefield of biomes and people
a frontier of summer and winter rains
where karoo and coast, veld and forest
clash for space like colonists

the Gonaqua, the Ndlambe, the Gqunukhwebe
led their cattle here before abelungu
Strandlopers knew the sea and mountain paths
to wilde dagga and impepho like their own voices

Rhini, place of reeds,
where yellow finches wove their nests
        consternation when the pale ones arrived!
        stuttering guns tore the Milky Way open!

the crown of thorns on Makana's Kop
drove the valley red with madness
              red the autumn leaves dipped in blood
              the river iQohi carved sjambok-lashes into the soil
              iQohi! Kowie! iQohi! Kowie!

        the rain will return
        (we must believe it)
        to rock and shrub, trickling down
        to the roots of grass and hearts of vygies
        the earth's hands are always open

*

I look up at the Settler's Monument:
ugly hull, death ship in the mist
plowing through the mountain
        through the trek routes of iinkomo
to and from the Zuurveld
        the sweetest grass in summer
sour and bitter winters
        the taste of grass composed
the stomping of hooves and feet

trekboers knew this too:
don't stay too long lest you fuck up a place
but greed poked out their eyes
turned their mouths into murders of crows
who flew with death in their beaks
across this bitter land

*

before the "Battle of Grahamstown"
Makhanda ka Nxele had a vision:
their bullets would turn to water
but Elizabeth Salt betrayed the prophecy
she passed through the amaXhosa
with a baby on her back
kanti the water in her womb
        was gunpowder she smuggled
        to feed the British cyclone

until a thousand bodies lay strewn across the hills

water!   finally
                warm and streaming from their bodies
        dipped the reeds in sorrow
euphorbias shed yellow flowers on the banks

their blood did not run free to the sea

                *

I climb the koppie next to P. J. Olivier
        the sun sleeps in after all the infernos
the N2 cuts like reins through fossilised rock
to restrain hurried petrol bombs on wheels

        thick mist engulfs the town
                just me and the crowd in the veld
they want to lead me through this war
        they want to be my water

but I extinguish nothing
        we just sway together
to and fro
        ageless beings
to and fro
        in the choking mist
on the crowded hills of Makhanda

stoke
new south wales, december 2019

the sun's pink dim dot is veiled in mourning soot
for weeks she blankly stares, her only eye refuses to cry
the waterfall forest we visited last month burns to the ground
the searing glow of flaming walls, an army of blowtorches
they singe they sing meters high into the sky age-old witnesses
of rain and bark fall one after the other and subside horizontally

no one hears their xylem explode
hears the whimpers, the breaking hoarse cries
kangaroos and pythons flee without finding green
the stench of burnt hair, millions of spirits surrender
they billow like the heat – the mountains smoke them out

we fill the car with petrol and speed
across smouldering hills to the ocean
the scorched remains of mosquitos and bees
koalas and dingos goannas and bush turkeys
arrive with us at the river's mouth
we breathe in the dead
breathe them out
and in

the lungs outside our lungs
become cinders
we devour slap tjips beneath
a vengeful sun
she writes pink love letters
in the waves full of ash

for the crowds in the wind
and the water
the crowds in our hair
and in our blood

and she refuses to shed
a single fucking tear

flakes

> *he will not see me stopping here*
> *to watch his woods fill up with snow*
>
> – Robert Frost, "Stopping by Woods on a Snowy Evening"

oil by-products and PFAS sift through all living things
gathering in the nooks of cells
corpuscles tumbling through our tubes
occupying our internal waters

quite poetic that the waste of global highways
penetrates and courses through us like cars
snow melts and turns transparent
but this technicolour stain is forever

spine-chilling, fellow traveller:
as you read these words
they're already sprouting toxic shrooms
in the dark folds of your flesh

the most carefree dream about my dad in years

you stand younger, less arthritic
the lines lighter across your face

in a free state field behind a .30-06
eland in your scope, finger on the trigger

khaki jacket zipped to the chin
your smile vast and oracular as the sun

I run towards you, the buck jolts
your mouth overcast for a moment

your long-gone hunter's dreams
but rays break through when you see me

the sky blesses us with flocks of hadedas
flamingos pelicans african greys

they land around us like a queer quilt
fold their wings together like a homecoming

to my parents

if you die in the rain
may the sky wash you with its showers
may the heavens wail and zinc roofs tremble
keep your mouth-eyes open till the end
slowly drink in the dying light

don't worry about us – you raised us
on mieliepap and the children's bible
we'll be fine

rather recall the tenderness
of your supple bodies
the hills you scaled together

those sandstorm sunsets
when ink swallows returned
to write love notes
on the purple page of the night

disappear

we're walking somewhere outside mcgregor
a protea farm against the mountain slope
slabs of drunken rock fall and wreathe into valley
a wall of clouds boulders in like gossip

we take in the langeberg
the peaks are islands in a sea of vapour
licking at our limbs we climb out
of ourselves inhale the scentless mist
we are wiped out –

the shards of earth know this vanishing
they'll scrape against the blue ceiling
and retreat in slow motion
until the earth becomes flat again
and clouds gather once more
as if no mountains ever lived here

mountain indaba
overheard from an Apu, with thanks to LM and AC

one day the mountains shook
their roots loose and started walking
some slid easily from the soil
others dragged cities along

Apu Pitusiray prepared the Sacred Valley
for their arrival in Peru
the Apus unfolded a prairie
the Vilkanota sailed closer

the Himalayas and Alps sent their delegations
Hoerikwaggo and Kilimanjaro were called in
consultants from the Caucasus…
vertebrae from the Cordilleras…

the gatherers cleaved their way open
throwing oceans around
their wake flooded coastal towns
scattering people like anchovies

the mountain herd multiplied
drowned their drought in the Vilkanota
and slowly took their seats
their bodies filled the dusk

when the sun went down they lit the sacrifice
donated all the fuel themselves:
forests and houses, fields and farmland
anything combustible that smelt of ruin

the summits huddled together
to feel the heat against their frozen foreheads
the ancient story of decay
danced in their cavernous eyes

the cries from their stone laps grew into chants
thundering through the chasms of canyons
the planet trembled one last time like the day
when the first mountain rose from the sea

the earth envoy went to bed
and woke up to a charcoal day
dusted off the soot, echoed their goodbyes
and set off to their quieter homes

ode to air

the wind brings you back to me, dear air
you always elude me, always everywhere
you don't discriminate between covid
and teargas: diffusion is deeply democratic

the wind unveils your hidden ocean
you ripple through the guava tree, the bougainvillea,
my hair and the thirsty fields of grass
on the dry hills of makhanda

you carry all things unfit for gravity
you are our sensory wifi, the epically invisible
conductor of heat, the stench of death
purveyor of pollen and phosphorous

I want to be more like you, air
you resist neither clouds nor missiles
come blow away my fury, carry my voice far
flood my battered lungs, o blood-sweet air

if I wake before I die
andahuaylillas, peru

if I wake before I die
I'll go out and fill my lungs
with the scent of earth
after a long night's rain

I'll squat on my haunches
in a cornfield's morning light
coffee steaming like a heart in my hands
the sparrows' shadows shooting arrows overhead

I'll walk up to the mountain
feel the caffeine pulse in my temples
the wind will blow my skull clean
and I'll take a good look at my dying self

I'll caress the spring grass
the far blue peaks the bright valley
all the grateful glimmering rocks
and I'll come back down with the dogs in tow

walk back home
snuggle under the far blue duvet
and thaw my bones
in the heat of your skin

a corpse is also a garden

I know for certain
my body or the world will desert me
horribly or quietly my heart will come to a stop
and I'll become a garden for the fungi that sprouted me

the buffet of my cells will flourish elsewhere
the mouths of hungry flowers scream on the koppies
the valleys yawn to swallow me whole

but for now I'm a sweet thorn tree on feet
spilling words like small yellow flowers
for now I'm a donkey gorging on shopping bags
a flock of hungry hands, a whirlpool, a thunderstorm
and one day, thank god, I'll be done

my mouth no longer this muddy membrane
this traffic jam of swear words, carbohydrates and breath
I'll turn into a gateway for the bugs to carry me away
and finally, I'll feel at home on earth

SOUTH AFRICAN POETRY SINCE 2014

— RECENT RELEASES —

Owele by Sihle Ntuli

Rootbound by Manthipe Moila

Fall Risk by Kobus Moolman

Poetry NonScenes: New performance poems beyond the Struggle,
edited by Tom Penfold, Adam Levin and Deirdre Byrne

Dayspring: A Memoir by C. J. Driver, edited by J. M. Coetzee
A 2024 *NEW STATESMAN* BOOK OF THE YEAR

The Book of Unrest by Nick Mulgrew
SHORTLISTED FOR THE 2024 NIHSS AWARD FOR BEST POETRY

A Short Treatise on Mortality by Douglas Reid Skinner

Peach Country by Nondwe Mpuma
SHORTLISTED FOR THE 2023 NIHSS AWARD FOR BEST POETRY

— RECENTLY-AWARD-WINNING TITLES —

Ilifa ngu Athambile Masola
WINNER OF THE 2022 NIHSS AWARD FOR BEST POETRY

An Illuminated Darkness by Jacques Coetzee
WINNER OF THE 2022 INGRID JONKER & OLIVE SCHREINER PRIZES

All the Places by Musawenkosi Khanyile
WINNER OF THE 2021 NIHSS AWARD & 2020 SALA FOR POETRY

Everything is a Deathly Flower by Maneo Mohale
WINNER OF THE 2020 GLENNA LUSCHEI PRIZE FOR AFRICAN POETRY

AVAILABLE FROM GOOD BOOKSTORES IN SOUTHERN AFRICA
UHLANGAPRESS.CO.ZA

www.ingramcontent.com/pod-product-compliance
Lightning Source LLC
Chambersburg PA
CBHW070206100426
42743CB00013B/3076